Special Message
Maxine Edmunds

At the age of three, my husband Larry lost his right arm in a trolley accident. Instead of becoming bitter he continued to trust in God and his divine purpose. I've always admired this about him and I was so pleased when I learned he was ready to share the most pivotal moments in his life.

May the words contained within the pages of this book inspire you to continue no matter what setbacks you will experience. Challenge yourself to live the life you want.

The Destination After The Devastation

One Hand
Left Hand
In A Two Hand
Right Hand World

By
Rev. Dr. Larry Edmunds

*Ray & Sharon,
You have lead a life
of service and dedication to the
ministry of Jesus — You are a joy!
Your uncle
Larry Edmunds*

The Destination After The Devastation:
One Hand, Left Hand, In A Two Hand, Right Hand World

Narrated & Written: Larry Edmunds with Trish Geran
Editor: Trish Geran Co-editor: Maxine Edmunds
Cover & Typography Layout: Trish Geran

Edmunds, Larry
Autobiography
1. Edmunds, Larry, 1939-
2. Surviving the loss of an arm at age 4
3. Growing up in Black Pittsburgh 1940s-1950s
4. The Blenders
5. The Marcels
6. Lincoln University late 1950s to early 1960s
7. Omega Psi Phi Beta Chapter (Charlotte "Lottie B." Wilson)
8. Gangs in Germantown, Philadelphia
9. St. John's Baptist Church in Woburn, MA
10. President Joseph-Désiré Mobutu

Contents

Prologue

My mother told me that I was a difficult birth. My arrival came at a time when her doctor was on vacation. I had great difficulty breathing. This beginning set a pattern for my formative years, and one of those tragedies was the near death encounter with a trolley car.

I have so much to be grateful for. In this presentation, I have attempted to say "thank you" Lord for lifting me to a level of seeing how I have been able to overcome my circumstances.

Over those experiences something greater than me guided me through my many adventures in life. The physical loss of my right arm meant making my way was from tragedy to triumph.

I'm grateful for God's grace. Hopefully you can find a light on your pathway as I have found on my journey through life.

Dedication

This book is dedicated in loving memory of my parents Hattie Mae and Richard Edmunds and my siblings: Lillian, Bob, Betty, Nettie, Billy, Martha, and Norman, who played significant roles in my life.

Chapter One
My Bridge, My Family

Honor your father and your mother,
that your days may be long upon the land
which the LORD your God is giving you.
Exodus 20:12

I was born in 1939 in Pittsburgh, Pennsylvania. My mom, Hattie Mae Staley, was from North, South Carolina, located in Orangeburg County, and my dad, Richard Vernon Edmunds, was from Sutherlin, a small town near Halifax County in Virginia. She was 17 and he was 22 when they met in Pittsburgh in 1923. Shorty after they married.

My mom was proud of Orangeburg County. It was named in honor of William, the Prince of Orange, the son-in-law of King George II of England. The first church was of Lutheran denomination but was later changed to Episcopal. During the Civil War, it was utilized as a small pox hospital by Union General William T. Sherman. Although Sherman declined to

Front L-R: Mom Hattie Mae, Larry, Lillian, Martha, Norman, and Pop Richard Vernon Edmunds.
Back L-R: Bob and Billy

employ Black troops in his armies, he later led campaigns that freed slaves from 1864-1865. They called him "the second Moses or Aaron."

My dad, on the other hand, boasted about Virginia for some strange reason. One day, someone asked if I would rather be a dead dog or live in Virginia. I said, "A dead dog."

His hometown of Sutherlin was located approximately 15 miles from Millionaires' Row in Danville. It is where Major and Mrs. Sutherlin opened their home to Confederate President Jefferson Davis for one week. Today, Danville is known as the "Last Capital of the Confederacy."

There were "50 Shades of Blackness" in my mom and dad's family. Our complexions ranged from basic Black to almost White. My grandmother was half-White and Black, and my grandmother Ella Staley was mixed with Native American and African. When I was a kid, I remember my mom told me how she

The Edmunds Family

would carry a pouch around her waist that contained every cent she earned from domestic chores and picking cotton in the fields. And how my grandfather leased land to poor White folks. They were entrepreneurs in their own special way.

My sister Lillian was the first born followed by the twins, Netty and Betty. Sadly, they both died within a year. My mom said it was caused by an inexperienced midwife but she never wanted to give any details because the memory of it all served as a reminder of severe pain. Another possible cause could have been due to the small pox virus. At the time, an epidemic was declared in the United States.

When my mom took Netty and Betty to the doctor, he said their body temperatures were high, which made them unable to fight off an infection that might have been incubating but now active within the body. His advice was to put them in a wicker basket and place it in the windowsill. He was hopeful that the

Grandma
Ella Staley

16

cold weather would reduce the fever and restore their health. I might not know what happened to my twin baby sisters, but I do know about the day it happened.

When my mom was pregnant with the twins, one morning, she took the train to North, South Carolina, to visit folks back home. During her stay, she suddenly went into labor and a midwife was contacted. She delivered the first girl, Netty without any complications, but when she discovered Betty was in there waiting to come out, she panicked and possibly incorrectly cut the cords. Mom said she was not trained to handle the procedure of twins, which were at that time considered high risk. She was only trained for single births.

When I was a little boy, practically every family had a young child die during childbirth, shortly after birth, or from health complications. It was a norm especially in Black families.

There were 14 siblings in my mom's family-11 girls and 3 boys. Two of the girls, Ellen and Rosa, died.

The Staley Sisters
Front L-R: Eliza, Maggie, Etta, Colena, Hattie Mae.
Back: Addiebelle, Evangeline, Nancy, and Ella Mae

Ellen was very young and Rosa was in her 20s. Details about how they died were never volunteered. I would like to assume it was from natural causes.

Although the death of the twin girls took a toll on my parents, they continued to have six more children: two girls (Lillian and Martha) and four boys (Bob, Billy, Norman, and me). I was the youngest.

I grew up on the North Side of Pittsburgh in a moderate sized house located on Buena Vista Street. My childhood friends were Italian, Greek, and Jewish. The neighborhood was a diverse mixing pot. Issues like immigration and acts of injustice were not topics discussed around the dinner table. Either the Jim Crow legal laws were resolved in my surroundings or secretly hiding in unknown places. In other words, I never saw a "For Whites Only" or "For Colored Only" sign in the North Side of Pittsburgh.

My grandfather Richard worked on the railroad, and my dad was a chauffeur for a wealthy White man named, William Kerr Stamets.

Dad was responsible for driving Mr. Stamets wherever he wanted to go and for the maintenance of the car. He lived in the house on the third floor and his space was nothing short of a three-bedroom apartment. Every weekend, he would drive to Pittsburgh to visit us and sometimes on weekdays. It depended on what errand or chore Mr. Stamets needed him to do.

Mr. Stamets lived on a country estate in Mars, Pennsylvania, which was about 20 miles from Pittsburgh. He sold special machinery and tools to the steel mills.

Production of steel began in 1875. In the early 1900s, during WWI, ambitious Black Southern migrants were recruited, and by 1911, the city was producing half the nation's steel. Industrialists such as Andrew Carnegie, Henry Clay Frick, Andrew W. Mellon, Charles M. Schwab, and George Westinghouse built their fortunes in Pittsburgh, which was at that time referred to as "Steel City."

The William Kerr Stamets Estate

Pop Richard with Mom Hattie (left) and Aunt Lena standing by the Cadillac stretch limousine he drove for Mr. Stamets.

When my dad started working for the Stamets, Mrs. Stamets was in a nursing home. Periodically, he would drive Mr. Stamets to visit her. Bernice, the housekeeper, would prepare a special lunch for the trip and pack more than enough food to share with Mrs. Stamets.

Bernice was the maid, cook, purchaser, and "all of the above." She, along with her two children, lived in a spacious apartment on top of the garage. She was in charge of the daily upkeep of the house. Harvey, the man in charge of the farm, lived in a house that was located on the Stamets' estate.

I was a little boy when I met Mr. Stamets' two teenage children, Grace and Bill. His sister, Mrs. Dickerson, was a spinster and she lived there to help raise the children.

In the midst of World War II, Mr. Stamets had to lay off my dad due to financial restraints. He was rehired at his old job driving a truck and delivering meat for J. Guyer Ellison. After the War ended in 1945,

Mr. Stamets rehired dad. The Stamets and Ellison families were thoughtful and very kind-hearted.

My dad was Mr. Stamets' confidante and a close friend. When dad retired, he made sure to keep in touch. When Mr. Stamets died, he left dad a substantial amount of money and the stretch Cadillac. Dad converted the Caddy into a limousine service. He drove people to special events, funerals, and weddings. I guess that sense of ownership just naturally runs in the family.

Chapter Two

A Trolley To Dismember

*And they said, Believe in the Lord Jesus,
and you will be saved, you and your household.*
Acts 16:31

One of my fondest childhood memories is hanging out with my grandfather, Dempsey Staley. When I was around three going on four, he lived with us for a short period of time. In fact, he made it a point to do this with all of his children.

West Park was located a few blocks away from the house. We would walk there then sit on a bench that overlooked Lake Elizabeth and one that was close to the railroad track. We would watch the trains go by; I felt like I was floating on a cloud when I was with him.

The trains would pass by carrying heavy loads of appliances, cars, and coal. I was so amazed at how heavy the loads were, my mouth would fly open.

Left-Grandpa Dempsey Staley and Uncle Herbert Staley

Grandpa Dempsey would recall stories about his family and growing up in the Deep South. He told me that his brother, Uncle Herbert, served in World War II and was a truck driver for a special division called the Red Ball Express. It was created to keep the surrounding troops fully stocked with food, gasoline, ammunition boxes, and medical supplies. Often times, the weather or the possibility of surrounding enemy units made it impossible to travel to where life sustaining items were stored. It just wasn't safe. So a convoy of trucks, travelling approximately 20 miles an hour (at a snail's pace) were sent. There were no street lights on the road; there were no head lights on the trucks.

It has been noted that 75% of the drivers were Black. The only choices they had in the army was either be a driver, regardless of the enormous danger it imposed, work in the mess hall, or in the laundry.

One day, when Uncle Herbert was driving on the Red Ball Express highway, suddenly a bomb exploded under his truck. He was thrown a few feet and landed face down. It was a miracle that all of his body parts remained intact. He was traumatized of course but was back on his job the next day.

Shortly after Grandpa Dempsey came to live with us, he was diagnosed with cancer. My mom said to only ask him to do tasks that required little physical effort.

There was only one place I wanted Grandpa to take me, and that was the John Heinz History Center. It was located on the North Side next to the H. J. Heinz Plant.

I wanted to learn about the exhibitions, From Slavery to Freedom, and the Underground Railroad, which are said to be beyond educational. Grandpa Dempsey said that Blacks survived horrific times and I wanted to feel the words that always caused his eyes to well up.

During the 1800s, Pittsburgh was a major stop for the Underground Railroad, the most impressive method of activism utilized to free slaves. Harriett Tubman was the conductor, and the men in Pittsburgh who helped influence their escape to Canada were: Lewis Woodson, a barber, educator, and minister; John B. Vashon, the richest black man in Pittsburgh; and John Peck, owner of the downtown Oyster House. Slaves who didn't reach the other side to a safe house settled in the western and northern areas of Pittsburgh.

As I mentioned earlier, my happiest days when I was a kid was hanging with Grandpa Dempsey. My saddest was when a trolley accident almost claimed my life.

It was spring in Pittsburgh and the weather was warm but pleasant. I remember how excited I was when I learned I was going to the store with my sister Martha. She was 7 years older so I felt like I was with my second mom when I was around her.

At that time, my cousin Evelyn Strickland was in charge of looking after us until my mom returned from Philadelphia. She was attending a convention with her congregation, Church of God, a world-wide denomination that was founded in Cleveland, Tennessee.

L-R: Norman, Martha, and Becky, my neighbor. I was holding the Bible a few months before the trolley accident.

It had been a week and Martha sensed I was getting a little restless so she thought some fresh air and a walk to the nearby store would help calm me down. Her friend Kathleen Coleman and our little cousin Joanne went along with us.

Stores in communities were referred to as "mom and pop." Most of the owners resided above the store. It was where they worked; it was where they lived. Perishables and basic household items were sold. Some owners allowed items to be bought on credit, and for a penny a day you could check out a book. But my favorite part of the store was the ice cream counter, which was located in the back.

Martha shopped for a few personal items and as soon as she was finished, Joanne and I ran to the counter and ordered a cone with two scoops of vanilla ice cream.

I was so preoccupied with entertaining myself the cone tilted slightly, but I made sure it returned to its original form. We walked outside and the exposure from the heat caused the ice cream to melt. I managed but

Joanne's napkin was saturated. When Martha noticed the near disaster, she released my hand to clean around her cone. Suddenly, I turned and ran away from her, without realizing a trolley was coming. That is the last thing I remembered. When I finally gained consciousness, I was in the hospital.

My brother told me details of what happened. He said I was hit by a trolley car and landed underneath the rear wheels. A White minister named Reverend Hoover crawled under and prayed for me. When the emergency crew came, they had to wait until a trolley car arrived before they could jack up the side and remove me.

I was taken to Allegheny General Hospital Emergency Room. He said he and dad watched as the nurses and doctor attempted to untwist my legs, and work on the rest of my body. My wrists were smashed, my insides were disemboweled, my legs and arms were broken, but because gangrene had set in the right arm, they had to amputate around my elbow. It was a miracle I survived.

Grandpa Dempsey Staley

My mom returned early from her church conference in New Jersey. She walked in my hospital room holding her worn Bible with scriptures already bookmarked that pertained to restoration of health and trusting in God.

When Grandpa Dempsey found out about the accident, he was stricken with grief. He wanted to carry my pain and that made me sad. It was no secret-I was one of his favorite grandkid.

A few months after the accident, Grandpa Dempsey died. The last time I saw him, he said to always remember...there are no accidents in life. I thought that was strange to say at the time, but I soon realized he was preparing me for this moment.

Chapter Three

It Passeth All Understanding

And the peace of God,
which passeth all understanding,
shall keep your hearts and minds through Christ Jesus.
Philippians 4:7

After months that seemed more like years of being confined to the daily routine hospital visits, tests, and therapy, I was finally released to go home. I would miss the sweets and cute nurses, but it was time to find out what was waiting on the other side of my new "normal" life. My mom was strong and the few talks we had in the hospital prepared me to handle any situation that may leave me speechless or extremely uncomfortable.

During my entire stay in the hospital, my mom was calm and dad was cool. They contained their emotions, a skill many Blacks in those days practiced. It was a must to display a show of strength for the sake of the family's well being.

Even after the accident, I continued to attend church with Norman and Martha, and hold the Bible close to my heart.

My mom didn't want me to label myself as being handicap. She wanted me to concentrate on the value of life and less on the arm and I did just that. I began to feel stronger, willing, and capable. And when I realized that we never had a family member who lost a limb, I started to feel special and unique because I was the first.

She used to watch me play with the children in the neighborhood and she noticed that I was a little off balance. She taught me how to place less emphasis on the right side, and how to practice taking more time than usual when doing chores and tasks. I needed to be more patient; this would be the key. I put together a routine to generate more balance, but in time, the problem corrected itself.

When I was nine years old, we moved from 1209 Day Street and back on Buena Vista Street but at 1232. The house was larger in every way imaginable. It had four bedrooms, a living and dining room, a basement, and in the back was a two-car garage.

The Tabernacle Baptist Church was in the middle of where my old house was located, and Allegheny High School was on the far side of the park. My new home became my sanctuary.

Every morning, before I walked out the door to go to school, my mom would recite a scripture that would increase my confidence and strengthen my faith. I grew stronger, and I began to do kid things like never before.

I would roller skate with a group of children from the community. The rink was located in the basement at the Avery Presbyterian Church located on the Upper North Side. The one major problem was when the soot from the mills rolled in the city it would cover the floor. It was impossible to skate for long periods of time without falling, and in order to stand in place you had to hold on to the rails.

Our eyebrows and hair would be covered with gray dust. We looked like little white ghosts when we walked outside and our clothes reeked from the unusual smell from the soot.

Folks would remove their clothes off the line and shut all the windows. At times, the city would get so dark, street lights would come on at 10 a.m. The city would become so cloudy you couldn't see your hand in front of your face. It looked like the world was coming to an end. These types of incidents earned her the name "Smoke City."

The mills may have offered lucrative job opportunities that allowed people to advance their status of living to middle class, but the smoke from the mills was becoming an environmental hazard. We were used to it but we didn't want to accept it without a fight. When the politicians fell on numb ears about solutions, the residents started to relocate from the city to the suburbs.

I will forever be proud of some of Pittsburgh's historical accomplishments. In 1907-1965, it published the most widely read Black newspaper in the country, the Pittsburgh Courier. It urged Black voters to switch from the Republican to the Democratic Party and rallied Black support for World War II. It was where American Playwright August Wilson was born, and the home of Hall of Fame slugger Josh Gibson, and two of the greatest baseball teams of the Negro Leagues, the Homestead Grays and the Pittsburgh Crawfords. The Crawfords were owned by Gus Greenlee and they played in his baseball field, Greenlee Field, the first Black-owned, Black-built field in America.

Pittsburgh was the childhood home of jazz pioneers: Billy Strayhorn, Billy Eckstine, Earl Hines, Mary Lou Williams, and Erroll Garner. Eartha Kitt, Billy Holiday, Billy Eckstine, Art Blakely, John Coltrane, Charles Mingus, Mary Lou Williams, Chet Baker, Lena Horne, and Duke Ellington would frequent jazz spots like the Stanley Lounge and the Crawford Grill.

The Crawford Grill was also owned by Gus Greenlee and his business partner, Joseph Robinson. His son, William "Buzzy" Robinson, ran the club for 60 years. It was located in District Hill. The crowds were racially mixed, and if a jam session lasted until the wee hours of the morning, so did the audience. Just knowing that these movers and shakers once made their presence in my "backyard" inspired me to reach higher.

My brother Norman was four years older so when he left to join the military, I was the only sibling at home. My other brothers (Billy and Bob) and sisters (Martha and Lillian) were married. It was the best of all times. I had the run of the house and finally the chance to ask a lot of questions. Home was not only my sanctuary-it was now my place of refuge.

When I was 12 years old, I attended Cowley Elementary School. I joined the Boys Scouts and played on their baseball team. I was a pitcher and I struck out a lot of players. When I was needed outfield, I could play any of those positions as well. I could hit and I never struck out. I was good-I mean I really dominated the positions I played. And I give all the credit for my athletic abilities to men like Mr. Leonard, Mr. Kelly, and Mr. Moore. They encouraged boys in the

Me at 12 years old

community to play baseball and taught us how to be responsible young men.

I enjoyed the benefits sports brought to my life. I felt respected and admired by my teammates and yet humbled to the notion I could play any position.

This time of being the only sibling at home was both peaceful and comforting. But when Uncle Boyd came to live with us, I was happy to give it all up.

Uncle Boyd was my mom's brother and he made it a point to spend time with members of his family. When his wife died, he lived with Aunt Ella. She was known for baking cakes that were so delicious the taste remained in your palate for days. Why he chose to leave and replace coming home to that aroma for my long list of questions and places to go was besides me. We would hop on the trolley and tour historical sites in the city, catch a baseball game, or just sit and talk on the porch.

Uncle Boyd was a handsome guy, tall and lean with soft features. He worked at the Oliver Iron and Steel Corporation, which controlled the Allegheny and South

Side Railway through its stock ownership. He would never go out on weekdays. He left early in the morning and returned home after work to a home cooked meal by my mom.

One Friday, my mom and dad went to Farmers Market to purchase a few items. After Uncle Boyd took his nightly bath, he sat in the backyard. I heard this moaning and immediately rushed to make sure he was alright. When I opened the back door, he was regurgitating on the side of the house. He sat back down and continued to moan. He told me to call Odell, the funeral director, and to bring his new shoes.

I called my brother Billy, who lived nearby, but when I hung up the phone, mom and dad walked in the door. Billy drove us to the Divine Providence Hospital Emergency Room, which was located next to Allegheny High School.

It was a Catholic hospital and the nuns were impressed with how well dressed and groomed he was. A few days later, Uncle Boyd was gone.

When I got back home, I went into his room and fell in a deep slump like no other time in my life. I wanted to feel his presence and reminisce about the good times. I guess I wasn't ready to say goodbye. The idea seemed to be the right thing to do (to help fill the void) but I started to feel frightened.

I managed to spend another night in his room; it was the last time. The next day, I said my final goodbye. I slowly walked towards the door, looked back one last time, and gently closed the door.

Chapter Four

A Voice With A Name

Make a joyful noise unto the LORD, all ye lands.
Serve the LORD with gladness:
Come before his presence with singing.
Psalm 100: 1, 2

After Cowley Elementary School, I attended Latimer Junior High. They were both located on the North Side of Pittsburgh and in walking distance from my house. I enjoyed music class the most. It was where I discovered that I had a voice to sing tenor. This was when music and singing took a hold of me.

My mom had a beautiful voice. She would sing while doing chores around the house and in the car especially when we went on long trips.

I'll never forget when Martha was attending Allegheny High School, her music class came to Cowley Elementary to perform in our Christmas program. They wore blue robes and they sounded angelic and strong.

My Cowley Elementary School picture

When Martha graduated, she went to nursing school and became a psychiatric nurse. She married twice and had three sons. Her second husband, Dewy Bryant, a star football player in high school, taught me how to swim. He would play the piano and I would sing.

Martha was a giver and a progressive person. She always thought that she was my "mom." In fact, it was the last thing she said to me over the phone when we last talked. She died shortly after in September of 2017.

I attended the Northside Church of God and the Buena Vista Street Methodist Church. My dad's church, Mount Zion Baptist Church, was in Bellevue. After he retired, he attended quite often and sometimes he would accompany us to a Sunday service. Mom was serious about church. She didn't care who wanted to go. Her job was to make sure you had transportation to get there on time.

One day, before Sunday school, a visiting lady said to me that if I prayed right God would bless me and grow another arm. I said he did grow another arm-a spiritual one. This was just one of the many encounters I had and would experience.

In high school, during the 1950s, I was fully aware that Jim Crow segregation laws were the "law of the land" and separate was equal in most states, but the Pittsburgh public school system was integrated and the format mirrored the communities.

I continued to have White, Italian, and Greek friends in high school and we stuck together even when we were at odds with one another. If one of us would be in a fight with a White guy, and if a White guy from another area would try to help him out, "our" White guy would reject his help and take sides with the guy he was fighting.

I attended Allegheny High School in Pittsburgh, another school located near the house. The dances were one big party. We would have annual fundraisers by putting on productions of variety shows where people would sing and play instruments in front of the public, parents, and friends.

I joined a group called, The Blenders while I was in high school. I used to sing on the street corners like most children did in those days, until Walt Maddox, a singer with The Blenders, asked me to join the group. At the time I joined, the other members were: Walt Maddox, Charles Watson "Fuzz", Eddy Howard, and Melvin Glover. I sang tenor.

We continued to sing on the streets, in lounges on the North Side of Pittsburgh, and even in variety shows on weekends. We gained exposure when disc jockeys like Bill Powell, Barry Kaye, and Porkey Chadwick, would host Record Hops. They would set up at various locations and play your records. We would battle other groups to find out who was the "best of them all." It was an excellent way to make a few bucks.

Our musical director, Wilford Cotton, taught us how to sing in four-part harmony and how to stay on key. He choreographed our movements and played the piano while we rehearsed the songs.

Singing became therapy for me and it gave me a keen sense of identity. The attention was cool but mostly I enjoyed bringing special recognition to the community.

We recorded a song called, "Jitterbug." I think we sold one copy. We later recorded "Desert Sands", which received little response. We renamed the group, The Blanders, under the organization Clemw, Inc., which was derived from the first initials of our names (Charles, Larry, Edward, Melvin, Walt.) Soon after, we went our separate ways, and I continued to concentrate on completing the required classes for a high school diploma.

When I turned 18 years old at the end of my senior year, the Pittsburgh Railway Company made a financial settlement with my family, which included a prosthesis. I was fitted by J.E. Hanger–Orthotics and Prosthetics and received therapy on how to utilize my "new arm" to the best of my ability.

The Blanders L-R: Charles Watson, Walt Maddox, Larry Edmunds, Eddie Howard and Melvin Glover.

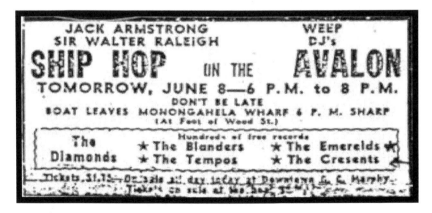

54

The trip to J.E. Hanger was an adventure for me; it was the time I was able to travel on my own. At that time, I was dealing with my physical difference, racial identity, and independence. I wore it only when I went somewhere special. I thought of it as an accessory.

One day, I was visiting a young lady and she demanded I take it off. "Be yourself!" she said with bold, street-like emphasis. Then she put it in an A&P shopping bag. It was then when I was convinced that I never had to over-compensate because I did not have a right arm.

For three years, I wore the prosthesis-off and on-regardless of the discomfort and distractions it caused. At times, it was the center of a joke. Today, it lays at the bottom of my best friend Sammy Jenkins' closet in Philadelphia, and to this day, he has never mentioned that "thing" to me.

My mom said that when the driver of the trolley that dismembered my arm would see her out in public, he would have an anxiety attack and would become so overwhelmed he couldn't complete his shift. He told her he accepted that he would be forever haunted by the accident.

If I was given a right arm today, I wouldn't know what to do with it. Not to sound ungrateful, but I honestly function just fine and I strongly feel it would complicate how I carried out my daily tasks.

Chapter Five

The Virtues Of Learning

The heart of the prudent getteth knowledge;
and the ear of the wise seeketh knowledge.
Proverbs 18:15

In 1958, I was accepted at Lincoln University in Lincoln University, Pennsylvania. It was the first Black College for Black men, where you could earn a degree. At that time, Lincoln was an all-male school. It became coed in 1968. It was once called the Ashmun Institute and was re-named in honor of President Abraham Lincoln in 1866.

My brother Bob drove me to Lincoln and my mom rode along to make sure I had a room in the dorm ready for immediate move in. It was about a five hour drive, and when we arrived, Mom was sad and acted as if she didn't care, but she shed a few tears. Then she said to make friends.

My dad was in the hospital so I almost delayed registration, but he insisted that I continue my journey and he promised he would continue his. He had some kind of a flu virus but no one wanted to ask him about it. They were afraid that it might be pneumonia. After a few weeks, he regained his strength and was released from the hospital.

For the most part, I was the only student in the dorm; the others were football players. And when they entered the hallway, you heard them loud and clear. The first weekend, guys who lived in nearby areas like Philly, Baltimore, and Harrisburg went home. The few that lived in far-away places like the east coast, the western part of Pennsylvania, and across the Mason Dixon line, stayed on campus.

I got home sick and called my mom. She said when you make friends ask if you could go home with them. The next week, a player from New York said he was going to Cheyney College to visit and I decided to tag along. When I saw all of those fine Black females I felt like I had found a new home.

Cheyney College was established for Blacks in 1837. It was initially called the African Institute, and in 1983, it became a university. It is not considered the "first" historic Black college because it was not a degree granting institution until after Lincoln was established.

In 1854, Lincoln University was founded by Jehudi Ashmun, a White social reformer and minister. He wanted to reorganize, preserve, and Christianize the Black Colony, which is now Liberia. The goal was to train Black men to go back to Africa and educate them.

When I attended, there were around five White men enrolled and they carried themselves as though they were Black. A White man in Chester County and female students who were either a professor's daughter or who lived in the community could attend Lincoln free of charge. Lincoln girls were tough like the guys.

All students were required to take math, science, liberal arts, biblical studies, Latin, Hebrew, or Greek, and music regardless of their major, a concept that was patterned after Princeton University.

In my music class, I joined the Glee Club. Every other week, we would pile up in a car and travel to an event center or Black college campus to perform Negro Spirituals, classical songs, and show tunes.

In my freshman year, I pledged Omega Psi Phi. And yes...we had to do whatever the existing members asked us to do.

Lincoln is home of the Omega Beta Chapter thanks to a woman named Charlotte T. "Lottie B" Wilson. Ms. Wilson lived in Lincoln University Village before there were dormitories on campus. At that time, it was where students lived, studied, and ate their meals.

When Ms. Wilson found out that Lincoln's administration turned down the Howard University representatives who wanted to form a second Omega chapter, she was livid. She told them to cancel their train trip back home, and she immediately initiated the second chapter in her living room.

Charlotte T. "Lottie B." Wilson

I was pledging when I met her. She was elderly and nearly bed ridden. All members on the line had to be approved by her. She was a priority to the Omega brothers. They cooked for her, and looked after her well being and safety. In 1935, she was made an honorary member of the Omega Psi Phi Fraternity. She was and still remains the only female member in the fraternity.

Charlotte Wilson lived in New York and relocated to Lincoln after she retired. Her husband, Mr. Wilson, was the main custodian on campus, and she was much older than he was. Ms. Wilson will always merit a place in my heart.

My pledge line was called the "Handicap 9" because each of us had some kind of physical disability. We had a championship wrestler who was blind named Rolland Clyde. I called him "Cheeks." In fact, I gave each pledge a nickname that represented who or what they resembled the most. You were nobody unless you had a nickname.

There was "Panda Bear" (Richard Pride Harrison) "King Dust" (Calvin Morris) and a few mice who were small in stature. I was "Captain Hook" and later became "Hooker." At first I didn't take to that name because of the manner in which I earned it.

One day during my first week on campus, James Jenkins, a freshman football player, offered to help carry my foot locker to my room. I told him that when I need a slave I would definitely let him know. He was furious. The next day, there was a pounding at my door. Someone had left a Black pirate caricature drawing of me as "Captain Hook." I humbled myself and went along with the nickname I rightfully earned. I hung the poster in the cafeteria so everyone could see it when they walked in.

I was a big rabbler on campus, which was someone who talked about you for what you didn't know or do. If you didn't know how to dress or answer a question in class, I would rabble on you. It was anything that was

I was the Commandant of the Omega Psi Phi
"20 Strong" line

off-point. For example, because Calvin didn't have a lot of clothes I named him "King Dust."

During the day, when the professors were on campus, Lincoln was a college, but after they left the campus, the students, particularly the varsity club and the fraternities, gave guidance to campus activities.

Lincoln had one of the largest percentages of Black doctor, lawyer, and minister graduates. Howard University and Meharry Medical College would also become comparable to these statistics.

Notable people who attended Lincoln were: Langston Hughes-poet, novelist, lyricist; Cab Calloway-musician, bandleader, singer-songwriter; Gil Scott-Heron-film score composer, poet, songwriter; and Thurgood Marshall-judge, politician. In 1967, Marshall became the first Black Supreme Court Justice.

Thurgood Marshall was also a rabbler on campus and on Capitol Hill. After he graduated, he continued his education at Howard University Law School.

I knew quite a few graduates from Lincoln who advanced their education at schools like Howard and Princeton, and Black teachers from the south who enrolled at institutions like Columbia and Princeton.

During the summer, I joined another Doo-Wop group called, The Marcels. They were formed in 1959, in Pittsburgh. The lead singer was Cornelius "Nini" Harp (Lead and Guitar) Ronald "Bingo" Mundy (First Tenor) Gene Bricker (Second Tenor) and after Walt Maddox (Second Tenor) Richard Knauss (Baritone) and after Allen Johnson (Baritone) and Fred Johnson (Bass).

In 1961, they recorded their first number one song, "Blue Moon." After the single charted at No. 1 on the Billboard Hot 100 for three weeks, charted at No. 1 on the UK Singles Chart, sold one million copies, and was awarded a gold disc, that's when I was asked to travel with the group. We toured from Boston to North Carolina headlining and performing in just about every entertainment venue you could imagine.

My dad was not against my singing career, he just felt that it would be wiser to concentrate on my schooling. He said my voice was a gift, but there are a lot of good singers and if he and Mom were to sponsor my singing career what would become of it if something happened to either of them. Who would I rely on for financial support and how do you cash in on the time you have spent? He then asked me if I thought my siblings would step in where he left off. I had no adequate answer to that question...and I still don't.

What an established time in my life. I was an Omega, I was performing with a successful group, and my image was getting me places with the ladies, but not with all of the professors.

There was one professor that really got me and that was Dr. Orin Clayton Suthern II, my music appreciation teacher. He was the only teacher who called me "Hook", and he was the first teacher to give me a failing grade.

Each student was given a woodwind flute instrument called a Recorder. We were required to play a tune. It had a thumb-hole for the upper hand and seven finger-holes: three for the upper hand and four for the lower. I told him that because I only have one arm this would be an opportunity for me to miss class. He agreed and said that instead I should write a report on Aaron Copeland. Copeland was referred to as "the Dean of American Composers." He was a composition teacher, writer, and conductor.

I was overly confident about the assignment so I waited until the last minute to write the report, a report that was obviously thrown together with no thought. In addition to that, I exceeded the number of times allowed to "cut" class. Those combined dumb acts earned me a failing grade.

Dr. Suthern explained that he had to give me a failing grade because it was what I strived for. He really showed me who was in charge. I just knew he was going to let me off the "Hook." After three years, I had to leave Lincoln because of my declining academic status.

At Lincoln, there were five professors in my department and all of them knew each student by their full names. I earned that "F" and I learned a valuable lesson-never underestimate the seriousness of any situation; seek counsel if you must.

At Lincoln, you are required to maintain a certain GPA and if you did not, they would send you back home to your momma in a minute. There was a long waiting list of people wanting to attend and they needed the class space for students who were serious about achieving an education.

I placed my singing career on pause. Today, Walt Maddox owns the rights to The Blenders and The Marcels.

I became a part-time student at the University of Pennsylvania (one of the oldest Ivy League schools) and Temple University, both located in Philadelphia. My grades were above average, but I was determined to graduate from Lincoln University. I transferred my credits back to Lincoln and continued where I left off.

I returned just in time to participate in the Omega Psi Phi Fraternity 50th Anniversary event. We invited our Omega brother, famed poet and writer, Langston Hughes, to be our guest speaker. Langston said that Lincoln University had invited him on numerous occasions, but when his brothers invited him, he had to accept.

Langston Hughes was the keynote speaker and I, along with three other brothers, was asked to speak about the four principles of the Omega Fraternity: scholarship, perseverance, manhood, and uplift. I spoke on scholarship.

After my speech, I was given an award. I was so surprised I was careful not to act so scholarly because I wanted to maintain my image as the "King of Rabble." When Langston Hughes stepped up to the podium, he mentioned a few of my points. I was on cloud nine the entire day.

Second-left, Langston Hughes, kneeling (L) me, and in middle with light colored trench coat is Jesse Jackson.

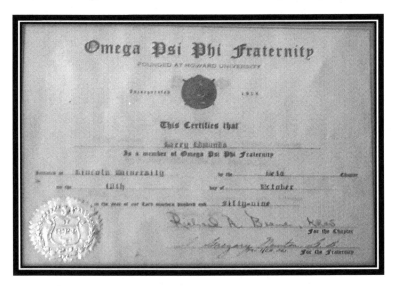

Civil rights activist Jesse Jackson was in attendance. I first met Jesse when the Glee Club performed at North Carolina A&T. He was on a football scholarship; his position was quarterback.

As a Second Vice Grand Basileus, Jesse Jackson held the highest rank position in the Omega Psi Phi Fraternity for an undergraduate on a national basis. He joined Dr. Martin Luther King, Jr. in the fight for injustice, headed organizations such as Operation Bread Basket (Chicago branch) Operation PUSH, and the Rainbow Push Coalition, and was a two-time Democratic presidential candidate. Jesse has always had a sharp mind.

I majored in history and in May of 1963, I graduated from Lincoln University. After I walked across the stage, my cousin opened the envelope I was so eloquently handed and nothing was inside.

I walked over to Professor Kuener's house on campus. He was the registrar and he also taught classes. When I arrived, he said to come in that his wife was

Lincoln University "Class of 1963" 50th reunion

about to serve him dinner. We walked over to the administrative office and he opened the safe. After he took my diploma out, he looked me straight in the eyes and said in his German dialect, "This is a handle that you can hold on to for the rest of your life."

I accepted a position as a juvenile probation officer with the County of Philadelphia. My colleague and friend Sammy Jenkins also applied and was offered a position. Sammy was my "right hand man" and the keeper of my prosthesis.

Chapter Six

A Greater Understanding

*Give to a wise man, and he will be yet wiser;
teach a just man, and he will increase in learning.*
Proverbs 9:9

I was as a juvenile probation officer and I also worked on a part-time basis with Upward Bound, a nationally known federally funded educational program that offered better opportunities for students to attend college. There was a heavy concentration on rural areas, low income families, and parents who did not attend college.

During the summer, I went home to visit my family. As I was walking out of a drycleaners, I bumped into a friend from my Pittsburgh neighborhood, Maxine Heard. She had just pulled up in a brand new Pontiac GTO with a glass muffler. When I told her what I was doing in Philadelphia, she said that she was working on her masters in Education at Duquesne University in

Pittsburgh. She needed first-hand information about what it was like working with troubled youth for her thesis. She didn't want to emphasize stats that she could find in a textbook or a police report. I also knew her from high school.

Maxine was teaching at Manchester Elementary School in Pittsburgh. She received an undergraduate degree at Cheyney University, was the president of the Graduate Chapter of Delta Sigma Theta, and the president of the Business Women Association.

Over time, Maxine and I became more than just friends. All this talk about statistics and ways we can make a difference in the world for our youth widened my eyes to what a nice and wonderful, beautiful young lady she was. One thing led to another and I knew without a doubt that the smartest thing for me to do next was to ask for her hand in marriage.

Maxine is no ordinary person. She had high standards and I always had such great confidence in her ability to achieve anything she set her mind to. She is a winner, not hard to please, self-determined, intelligent, "thinks" she has a sense of humor, and is emotionally strong. She doesn't compete with me. She is my better half versus my bitter half, she knows how to handle guys, and since the day we met not once have I had a problem with her.

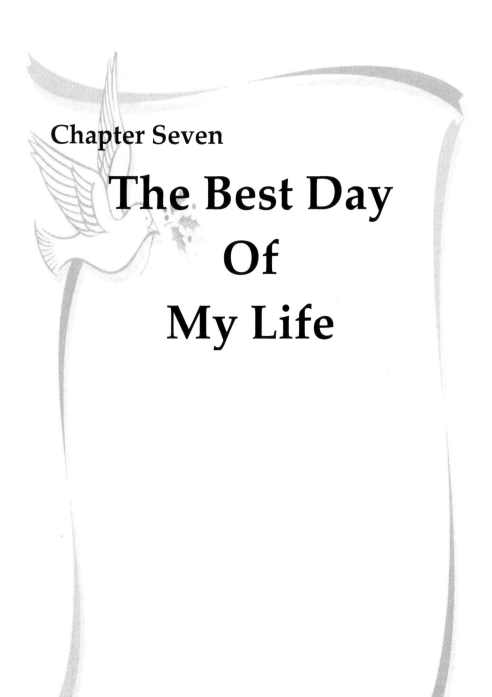

Chapter Seven

The Best Day
Of
My Life

He who finds a wife finds a good thing,
And obtains favor from the Lord.
Proverbs 18:22

In 1969, it was still customary to ask the parents for permission to marry their daughter. But a year ago, Maxine had loss her dad, John William Heard, Sr. (Pop Heard) so her mom Clara (Mom Heard) gave us her blessings.

Maxine was from a family of 10. And like my mom's family, the Staleys and my family the Edmunds, they loss two children at very early ages. When I met her, she had just weathered the loss of Pop Heard, her Aunt Jessie McCoy "Aunt Sis", and brother, Robert Lee Heard "Dusty." All losses happened in the spring of the same year.

We decided to get married in Pittsburgh at Victory Baptist Church on June 21. Pastor Lehman Bates of Victory performed the ceremony. My brother Norman

Clara and John
"Pop" Heard,
Maxine's parents

At table L-R: Betty, Maxine, John, Freddia. On sofa
Catherine, Lessie, Mom Heard, Robert, and Alice.

arranged the transportation through the Yellow Cab Company. Our guests came from all over the country. Once they arrived, they were taken to scheduled events even if they were not formally invited. Some stayed in nearby hotels, mainly the Roosevelt Hotel and some were just running late due to traffic.

It was funny watching six people emerge from a little cab, but Norman suggested there only be only four ladies at once so they wouldn't wrinkle their dresses. The weather in June was hot and humid, but it didn't stop us from styling and profiling like we were rich White folks and celebrities in our own way.

We had two wedding receptions: one was held at Cork & Bottle Garden Restaurant which was located in downtown Pittsburgh, and the other was in Mom Heard's beautiful garden. We partied all night long. It was so pleasing to see how well our families got along.

June 21, 1969, Victory Baptist Church

L-R: Sammy Jenkins and Pastor Lehman Bates

Max's sister Freddia and Sammy Jenkins

Pop Edmunds, Mom Hattie Mae, and Mom Heard

Second wedding reception was in Mom Heard's garden

On September 4th of the same year I was married, I lost my dad. It saddened me deeply, but I was grateful he was there to watch me marry the most wonderful woman in the world. In 1983, Mom Hattie Mae went home to be with her beloved husband of 46 years.

Chapter Eight

Germantown That Once Was

And be not conformed to this world: but be ye transformed by the renewing of your mind, that ye may prove what is that good, and acceptable, and perfect, will of God.
Romans 12:2

When Max and I returned to Philadelphia, I continued to work for the county as a juvenile probation officer. On a part-time basis, I accepted the executive director position with the Germantown Community Youth Project.

I was interviewed by Mrs. Josephine Price. She was not only a beautiful person she was a community leader with a compassionate heart and very competent. No one could "say it" like Mrs. Price.

Mrs. Price had seven children (three boys and four girls). She dedicated her life to the project's mission-to work with gangs in Germantown, Philadelphia.

Germantown was once a middle-class Black community. During the 1940s, it was quiet and peaceful

Mrs. Josephine Price

and virtually no crime. There was never a reason to have keys to the front door because it was never locked. It was a rich and tight-knit community. Today, it continues to be plagued by gang violence.

Max and I shortened our honeymoon to attend Camp Teen Haven in York, Pennsylvania. She wasn't sure what to expect, but she connected quite well with the children.

Fighting and killing each other over material things, retaliation, and claiming territories, while dressed in nice clothes and shoes was the behavior of the gang members. It was about acts of intimidation to gain respect from everyone they encountered.

I guess in all of our lives, we experience certain counter reactions that force us to protect our reputation. It wasn't luck that enabled me to make it through traumatic events. It was the grace of God and I needed to find out His reason for me being.

Chapter Nine

Destiny Awaits

Instruct the wise and they will be wiser still;
teach the righteous and they will add to their learning.
Proverbs 9:9

In 1969, I enrolled in the Urban program at Gordon-Conwell Seminary in Philadelphia, to pursue a masters degree in theology. The school's mission was to prepare Christian leaders for various levels of ministry. I was preparing myself for ministry, not to be a pastor.

While attending Gordon-Conwell, I was the Director of African American Society at Salem State College, in Salem, Massachusetts. My duties included working with students and the administration.

I encouraged Maxine to apply for a job at the college. She interviewed with the department of education and was hired as an instructor.

The students at Salem felt strong about my mentoring and they showed it by waiting outside my office for hours. I was up-front and frank and they

Gordon-Conwell Theological Seminary

In my office at Salem State College

Dr. Daniel Nussbaum, friend and co-worker at Salem State College Social Work Department

appreciated that because most of them had been sold a bunch of "wolf tickets" for most of their lives. I wanted to teach students and demonstrate to the best of my ability how to develop their own understanding and intellect.

There were only a handful of Black students at Salem State College, which was quite remarkable because the first Black to graduate was Charlotte Louise Forten in 1856.

At that time, Salem State was called Salem Normal School and its mission was to prepare young ladies to teach. Charlotte's grandfather, James Forten, was one of the wealthiest men of African descent in the new Republic. In 2010, Salem State College became a university.

After I concluded my studies at Gordon-Conwell, Max and I relocated back to Philadelphia. I attended the University of Pennsylvania to pursue a masters in social work.

Mom Hattie Mae and Mom Clara Heard at
Gordon-Conwell graduation

Chapter Ten

St. John's Baptist Church

Let the message of Christ dwell among you richly as you teach and admonish one another with all wisdom through psalms, hymns, and songs from the Spirit, singing to God with gratitude in your hearts.
Colossians 3:16

In 1974, after a series of telephone calls from Salem State College administration, I accepted an offer to become a faculty member in their social services department. One of my responsibilities included being a participant in the presentation process of guest speakers on campus.

Salem State would invite people to speak about their experiences in life and the crucial decisions they made while climbing the ladder of success. They thought it would inspire and encourage the students.

Our guests were all remarkable in their own way, but when Julian Bond (politician, professor, activist, writer) walked on campus, it felt special. You see, Horace

Mom Hattie Mae and Julian Bond

Mann Bond, Julian's dad, was the first Black president of my alma mater, Lincoln University.

One day, my student Karen Turner Howard informed me that her church, St. John's Baptist Church in Woburn, Massachusetts, was in need of a pastor and she wanted to recommend me for the position. I was open to the possibility and followed through with a phone call. At first, I was hired as the supply minister, and then in 1976, I became the pastor. There were approximately 20 regular attending members, and two deacons: Walter Green and Plummer Turner. St. John's Baptist Church was fully organized in 1887.

The church needed a lot of repairs. I encouraged the members to be in prayer for the miracle that God had in store for the church, and then I established a relationship with each member so that we could move in the direction to repair and rebuild the facility.

I remember, after much prayer, sharing with the congregation we needed to expand the church facility to accommodate the potential increase of membership and

Mother Canada was St. John's
oldest and longest standing member

church ministries. We looked for land to build on but didn't have much success. We decided to stay and expand the church building on what I referred to as "holy ground", located on Everett Street in Woburn. Deacon John Womack Sr. (now Reverend Dr.) chaired the Building Committee. Deacon Neal Pearson (now Pastor) was the assistant chair of the Building Committee. Although there were many challenges, the work was completed in approximately one year.

We marched in the new building with prayers of thanksgiving to God for what only He could have done. Every obstacle was overcome with the entire congregation in prayer for this miracle. We were so blessed that the United Methodist Church in Woburn, led by Reverend William Flug, the pastor (aka Bill) and the congregation allowed us to occupy their church facility while St. John's building was under construction. I think we were there more than their members. They welcomed us with open arms and we were so thankful.

St. John's renovation. L-R: Lyndoors Grey,
John Womack, and Pastor Larry Edmunds

Inside of St.
John's structure
with John
Womack and
workers

St. John's first building renovation

To increase membership, I recruited members through outreach in the area and re-established a leadership structure with the board of deacons, trustees, choir, and musicians. I emphasized the need for the congregation to pray, to study God's Word, and to apply it in their daily walk. During the 1980s, the congregation grew both spiritually and in numbers, and the physical plant went through its first renovation.

In 1985, when I earned my tenure as a professor at Salem State College, St. John's Baptist Church began to play a larger role in my life. I resigned from my position at Salem State and focused solely on the ministry. I was so thankful to God for all He had provided.

I received an honorary doctorate from Shaw Divinity School and I felt complete. I had on my list of accomplishments two masters degrees, was very blessed with a supportive wife, a growing congregation, and the support of inspired ministry leaders. And as ironic as it may seem, when one of my members, Patricia Suber, was a little girl, she said that her pastor asked them to pray for a

St. John's Baptist Church & Sanctuary

Max and members of St. John's Baptist Church at the
Shaw Divinity School honorary doctorate ceremony

little boy who was hit by a trolley car in Pittsburgh. She was confident that boy was me. God has a way of bringing people together for His purpose.

Like I previously stated, I always believed that St. John's Baptist Church sat on "holy ground." For over 135 years, it was blessed as a place of divine worship, a place where many received Jesus Christ as their personal Savior, a place where people really became serious about their commitment to God, and a place people made a conscious effort to follow God's Word and mandates daily.

As I reflect back on the internal and external ministries, and our witness of God's love and ministry outreach to the Woburn community and beyond, I can see how the broader outreach of ministry impacted the lives of many today. The testimonies shared over these many years brought sweet joy to my soul. It's virtually impossible to write, within the pages of this book, all of the special moments and programs I was involved with as the pastor of St. John's. I can only share those, at an instance, that come to mind, and I give all the glory to Almighty God for making this possible.

I remember the weekly Sunday worship services and the teaching and learning opportunities i.e. Sunday School, Prayer/Share & Bible Study, the Friday evening Fellowship Dinners followed by Bible Study for the men, women, and youth. In the fellowship hall, we would close the Friday night Bible Study session holding hands while standing in a huge circle, thanking God, sharing prayer requests, and closing with a prayer. Watching how the youth, young adults, and seniors in that circle of love calling out prayer requests and concerns brought a sense of caring for one another. What a powerful feeling that was.

Then there was Church At Study (CAS) the Christmas events, Watch Night Services, the Seven Last Words, and Easter Sunday Worship Services (Resurrection Sunday). The Auxiliary Annual Days, and in the fall of the year, the Annual Revival Services followed by Homecoming on the following Sunday. "Young, Gifted &

Saved" worship services, led by Minister Henry Johnson (now Pastor Johnson) challenged the young adults with a renewed commitment of service for the Kingdom of God. The "Fantasies of Spring" Fashion Luncheon event, organized and executed by Juarez Farrington and committee. To see the children, youth, and young adults, and seniors model with great enthusiasm was quite wonderful. Such memories!

Ronald Walker and committee organized the Annual Reverend Dr. Martin Luther King, Jr. Luncheon. In some years, a youth project that researched Dr. King's contributions was put in place for the members at St. John's and the youth in the Woburn Community. The results from the projects were usually highlighted at the annual luncheon.

The Public Forum, under the leadership of Tom Farrington through a panel of expert professionals, focused on the issues of the community. The Forum encouraged people to be involved in their communities particularly in the areas of education and political concern.

The Annual Thanksgiving Dinner event, organized by Taryn Johnson and her committee, provided a place for folks from the community and the SJBC family to share a dinner and fellowship with one another. This potluck dinner made it possible for college students and folks from the community to come together to watch football, play fun games, or just have a great time.

I smile when I think of the very first "Café al la Soul" dinner organized and promoted by Tami Nash and her energetic committee. What an evening of fine dining with great food, and the music and Christian fellowship was really great. And when the parking lot across the street needed to be paved, George Sessions encountered a tree with deep roots, but he was determined to clear the debris regardless. I often spoke with him about this experience and how it impacted his Christian experience and his personal walk with the Lord.

There was also the Pastoral Anniversary program, Worship Services, and Birthday Celebrations. These services created a special time not just for me, but for

Visiting male chorus from Washington D.C. at
St. John's Afternoon Worship Service

the SJBC fellowship and other visiting churches. These special times strengthened a bond between SJBC and sister churches.

The Annual Church Reports, compiled by the Public Relations Department, captured a detailed report from every department, special committee, and special events held during the year. The bound booklet highlighted the ongoing history of the church. Carolyn Grey (now Minister) continues to update the history of SJBC by providing a historical accounting of St. John's 135 plus years of existence.

Organizations that impacted the SJBC Congregation, the Woburn Community and beyond, the ministry outreach from St. John's provided a Christian testimony of hope to some and reassurance to others. Those ministries, just to mention a few, were:

ESRA (Engineering Scientific Recourses for Advancement) organized by Dana Thompson, William Bagley, Mike Dawson and James Grisby. The engineers in the congregation came together to provide science based programs for communities in Woburn, Boston, and throughout Massachusetts. ESRA challenged the youth to excel in public schools. Their motto was "Engineering, A Workforce for the Future." ESRA encouraged many students to go into the field of science and technology after graduating from high school.

The National Council of Negro Women, Boston Chapter was organized by Carolyn Grey, a member of St. John's. This chapter was the first chapter in Massachusetts. The officers (Carolyn Grey, Corliss Thompson, Lois Collins-Gwinn, Esther Pearson [now Reverend Dr.]) were installed at St. John's Baptist Church.

The National Council of Negro Women, Boston Chapter install officers at St. John's.

The original "Young Americans." L-R: Nina Crenshaw, Larry Edmunds, Maxine Edmunds, Dot Lilly, Louis Crenshaw, Harriett and Henry Frisby (Not pictured-Bob Lilly)

Mary McCloud Bethune Institute, MMBI, was organized in 1991 by Esther Pearson (now Reverend Dr.). MMBI was a program for young girls that provided academic enrichment. Many women and girls from SJBC were very involved in providing teaching/learning experiences. Students enrolled attended classes on Saturday mornings from September to June of each year.

New Beginnings Christian Learning Center was a ministry outreach for preschool children. It was organized by the Board of Director members: Tesha Myers, Tamara Cadet, Patricia Suber, Wonjen Bagley, and Maxine Edmunds. New Beginnings provided a Christian based curriculum to young children at St. John's and students in the community who enrolled. I commend, for their service, this dedicated staff: Vivian Frye-lead teacher; Toni Walker-teacher assistant; and others who have supported this endeavor.

A mission tour trip that stood out was when Jonathan Mayo, in conjunction with The American Baptist Churches of Massachusetts (TABCOM) led a working mission tour to La Romana located in the Dominican Republic. The mission team included approximately 11 people from the congregation and they would spend one week doing mission work. They established a school, worked with the people to sure-up their homes, and provided clothing for the residence. The team worked in conjunction with Reverend Jean Luc Phanora, pastor of the Haitian Missionary Baptist Church. It was an eye opening

Some of the members of the St. John's Mission Team in
La Romana, Dominican Republic

experience for the 11 congregants who participated.

The Clean Water Mission Campaign, led by Dick Schaeffer (now Reverend) provided for earthquake relief victims. The entire congregation was involved by providing funding for this endeavor.

St. John's has been actively involved with The American Baptist Churches of Massachusetts (TABCOM) and the many ministry outreach programs for a number of years. One such ministry was the New Day program. This ministry dealt with young men and women who were physically and mentally challenged. New Day provided programs to support these young people, and it continues to thrive in the TABCOM experience.

Minister Darin Poullard (now Pastor) and his wife Vicki planned, executed, and chaperoned a trip for the first time to one of the National Baptist Conventions for the youth at St. John's. It was an adventure and learning experience for the chaperones and the teenagers. St. John's was closely associated with and participated in many activities of the Tri-State Convention (Massachusetts, New Hampshire, Rhode Island). We attended and participated in the mid-year session, the congress of Christian education, and the annual convention.

The Interstate Believers' Association was a ministry focused on family life and its daily challenges. This Association included teaching, preaching, fellowshipping, and worshiping. It provided a spiritual, uplifting experience. I was quite humbled and honored to receive the first Dr. Nathaniel Johnson Award for committed service to the Interstate Believers Association in 2005. This Award was in memory of the Association's first president, the late Dr. Nathaniel Johnson.

It is significant to first note that Deacon Paula Alexander (now Pastor) became the first ordained female deacon in the history of St. John's. She continues to be a valued asset to the ministry. The Deacons' Union and Ladies Auxiliary was led by Deacon Kevin Pearson. This national group was fortunate to have his leadership and dedication to assist people at the local, state, and national levels.

Coalition of Schools Educating Boys of Color (COSEBOC) was founded by Ron Walker. The purpose is to connect, inspire, support, and strengthen school leaders dedicated to the social, emotional, and academic development of boys and young men of color.

Innovators for Purpose, established by Mike Dawson, is a community outreach program that motivates young people to be innovative using their creative problem-solving skills. Its' focus is to cultivate an untapped source of innovators.

There were many special celebrations that took place in honor of St. John's. For the church's 100th anniversary, Benjamin Hooks (NAACP executive director, minister, attorney) was the keynote speaker, and former United States Secretary of State, John Kerry, was a guest speaker.

Former US Secretary of State, John F. Kerry spoke at St. John's Baptist Church "100th Anniversary"

L-R: Baptist minister and civil rights leader, Benjamin Hooks, was the keynote speaker at the church's "100th Anniversary." Pictured are SJBC members, Tom and Jurez Farrington.

Henry Lyons, former President of the National Baptist Convention, USA, spoke at my "25th Anniversary"

And for my "25th Pastoral Anniversary", Reverend Henry Lyons (former President of the National Baptist Convention, USA) was the keynote speaker.

In my 33 years as St. John's Pastor, there are four outstanding events that quite often cross my mind. The first is my "50th Surprise Birthday Celebration" that was held at the United Methodist Church, in Woburn, MA. I was surprised to see so many people, not just from across the Commonwealth of Massachusetts, but from all over the country. The dinner was catered, and the program was so moving I had to hold back the tears. I was even more surprised when the committee uncovered a baby grand piano, which was a birthday gift to me from the Edmunds and Heard families.

The piano was presented, in my honor, to the Music Department as a gift to the music ministry at St. John's. I am sure Mona Roberts, the Director of the Music Ministry was delighted. The tears started to flow; I couldn't contain them any longer. I could barely speak but somehow I

The St. John's Baptist Church baby grand piano was a
gift from the Edmunds and Heard families.

The Reverend Dr. Larry Edmunds Ensemble

blurted out a few words of appreciation. The piano was placed in the sanctuary where it remains today.

The second special event was when we were awarded the Lilly Endowment Grant, which was proposed by the Deacon Board and overseen by Chairman Deacon William Bagley. The purpose of this grant was to strengthen Christian congregations by providing opportunities for pastors to step away for a short time from the persistent obligations of daily pastoring and engage in a period of renewal and reflection (a time intended for exploration and reflection). What a blessing it was to meditate and reflect on God's call on my life.

Maxine and I traveled throughout the United States focusing on personal time for retreat, visitation with family members, former St. John's members and their churches. Our goal was to research the African American middle class and write about its impact on the church community.

We traveled to Jamaica to rest and enjoy the sights, culture, and the people. We visited the computer lab our

Missions Department set up as an outreach ministry from St. John's a year earlier. Denzil McKenzie, Esquire, a former member of Burchell Baptist Church-a historic church in Jamaica-made the connection between both churches and donated the computers, monitors, and equipment.

The Sunday prior to our departure from Jamaica, I had the opportunity to visit and preach at Burchell's morning Worship Service. The church was celebrating Harvest Sunday. What a time of great fellowship and sharing God's word to His people. Receiving the Lilly Grant was truly a tremendous blessing.

The third special event involved leading a delegation of pastors and religious leaders from the United States to Zaire, Central Africa. This experience was so incredible it deserved its own chapter in this book (Chapter 11-Mother of Civilization).

The fourth event was the Retirement Luncheon that St. John's members organized, and held at the Crowne Plaza Hotel, in Woburn, Massachusetts. After 33 years of service in this vineyard that the Lord assigned to me (and I must include my supportive and loving wife Maxine) was coming to a close. Many people attended from all parts of the country. It was truly a time of sadness and sweet joy all rolled into one event. I can still vividly see the faces of the people who had attended.

The keynote speaker was Reverend Dr. Calvin S. Morris, a longtime friend, colleague, and Omega Brother (Beta Chapter at Lincoln University). In fact, Calvin has participated in every major event in my ministry. For my ordination service at SJBC, Calvin preached a powerful message. He said, "My brother 'Hook'", as he always called me, "sit where the people sit. Hook, remember the gangs you worked with in Philly? So while pastoring at St. John's, remember St. John's is the SJBC gang." I remembered those words and made application in the ministry. I truly thank God for putting Calvin and me together through the good and sad times we have shared.

The Retirement Luncheon was almost over when suddenly the Luncheon Committee directed Max and me to the podium. Slowly, a sign was unveiled. It read, "Rev. Dr. Larry Edmunds Fellowship Hall." Max and I were stunned. We had no idea my name would last as long as the building exist. The sign was hung at the entrance of the fellowship hall.

The surprise of having something named in my honor is one of my highest achievements. Every time I think of that event, I am humbled, blessed and thankful to God for His calling on my life.

I was destined to be the pastor of a progressive church because I had professional administrative assistants; devoted diaconate (deacons & deaconess boards); trusting trustee board; Pastor's Aid Committee; church officers; ministry departments; ministry, missions & evangelism; finance & operations; music; Christian education; public relations; committee chairpersons; church choirs (Cherubs, Catherine Canada Youth Choir, Chapel Choir, Gospel Chorus, Men's Chorus, Reverend Dr. Larry Edmunds Music Ensemble); and members of the congregation.

Reverend Dr. Calvin S. Morris

The SJBC Women who were considered "Mothers of the Church" and who served with distinction were: Catherine "Mother" Canada, Betty Scott, Priscilla Coates Thomas, Bessie Horrigan, Dorothy Shivers, Delores Reed, and Lucile Hayes. My "Sons and Daughters" in ministerial leadership who, at some point, served at St. John's but who are now pastors, teachers, or retired from the formal leadership in ministry are: Rev. Dr. John Womack, Sr. (retired); Rev. Dr. Neal Pearson (current pastor of SJBC); Minister Harvey Hunt (deceased); Rev. Randy Fields (deceased); Rev. Eric Payne (retired); Rev. James Walker; Minister Cliff Parms; Rev. Toni Wilson; Rev. Richard Schaeffer; Rev. Michael Blackwell; Minister Robert Blakeney; Rev. Herman Nelson; Rev. Pickney Davis; Rev. Dr. Regina Shearer; Rev. Dr. Darin Poullard; Rev. Lyndon Myers; Rev. Henry Johnson; Rev. Paula Alexander; and Rev. Dr. John Page.

I would like to include so many more special moments and people be more detailed with the thoughts I have already expressed, but I probably would never complete this book. The aforementioned highlights are just a small sampling of my fondest memories.

I would like say to thank you to everyone who supported the ministry and for their capable and responsible leadership during my years as pastor at St. John's. To see and witness God's handiwork through each of you was a blessing that unfolded right before my eyes; a real joy to my soul. I thank God for the experience of using all of us.

The words from one of my favorite gospel songs, "If I Can Help Somebody" (written by Alma Bazel Androzzo) will always play a role in my ministerial journey. Words such as "I shall not let my living and my dying be in vain" are etched within my soul and has brought a deeper meaning to my life.

St. John's Baptist Church Family

For 135 plus years, St. John's Baptist Church has sat on "holy ground." For 33 years, it's been a place of divine worship where many received Jesus Christ as their personal Savior, and committed their lives to God to follow His word and mandates on a daily basis. As the pastor of St. John's, I was blessed in every way possible. I traveled to various countries on missions, and that included the mother of all civilizations, Africa.

Chapter Eleven

Mother
of
Civilization

Commit thy works unto the LORD,
and thy thoughts shall be established.
Proverbs 16:3

In 1999, Harvard University hosted a luncheon for President Mobutu of Zaire. As the pastor of St. John's Baptist Church, I attended along with several other pastors. Mobutu wanted to set the record straight about his reputation-for the mismanagement of his country-by adding his voice to a series of questions. During the luncheon, there was a protest going outside the building. Students believed he was a tyrant.

Professor and minister, Dibinga Wa Sa'id, from Massachusetts was in attendance. He introduced us to the President Mobutu. He was pleased to meet us and suggested we visit his country. Dibinga facilitated the arrangements; I was chosen to lead the delegation. Twenty-one members from various churches were chosen to travel to Zaire for 30 days.

Bishop Brown (R) and a participant at an event

Mobuto greeting his guests

Mobuto takes time for a photo.
I'm directly behind him

Zaire Fishing Village

Mobutu rose from poverty to the president of a country. In 1971, he renamed the Republic of Congo to Zaire.

Mobutu rolled out the red carpet the second we stepped off the plane. We felt like ambassadors in the "mother of all lands." Translators were assigned and every question was written down. We toured Central and West Africa in motorcades, and for the first time in my life, I felt close to what life must be like when one achieves respect coupled with power.

I will always remember floating on the Congo River, the second longest river in Africa, in Mobutu's yacht, which as you can see below was huge.

Touring historic sites. L-R: Dana Thompson, William Bagley, Pastor Edmunds, and Keith Clinkscale

At a state function in Zaire

Worship Service in Zaire

The people of Zaire waiting for the
second church service to begin

The opportunity to visit "Mother Africa" gave me the joy of a lifetime. And our return home to the United States gave us the extra exposure to visit the countries of Gabon, Togo, Ivory Coast, and Senegal. My life was enriched by these life changing experiences.

Chapter Twelve

Moving Beyond the Norm

I will feed My flock, and lead them to rest,
declares the Lord God.
Ezekiel 34: 15

After 33 years as the pastor of St. John's Baptist Church in Woburn, Massachusetts, Max and I sought direction from the Lord as to what lies ahead. Living in Danvers, Massachusetts, for 40 years, we knew that the cold winters were not for us. We were interested in retiring to a place with a warm climate and a practical place to live. After consideration of several possibilities, Las Vegas, Nevada was our final choice. Max and I firmly believed that God has a divine purpose for everyone's life.

Penny and Don Schricker, former members of St. John's, relocated to Las Vegas several years prior to our coming. They were instrumental in helping us find a house, which was next door to their place of residence.

Penny collaborated in the writing and publication of a journal called, "Journey Within–Moving to the Center of Your Growth." The journal is designed to help individuals make concrete application of Biblical principles in their daily pursuit. It is truly a ministry outreach, in that, it provides an opportunity for the reader and participant to capture their unique journeys as they seek guidance.

Prior to our departure from Massachusetts, we gave much thought and prayer to what God would want us to do in ministry. Upon our arrival in Las Vegas, we started an organization called L & M Global Outreach Ministry Consultants, LLC. The goal is to support ministries locally, nationally, and abroad. This LLC is an evangelistic mechanism to further the work of ministry.

Reverend Willie Davis was my friend and colleague. When he left Second Baptist Church, he organized Gethsemani Missionary Baptist Church (GMBC). He was diligent in this ministry and served as senior pastor until he was called home to be with the Lord in June 2009. I

Former
St. John's
members
and
neighbor,
Don and
Penny
Schricker

Reverend Willie Davis

believe God directed me to work with Reverend Davis in this newly organized ministry.

After much prayer, the Board of Directors, led by the Lord, extended a "call" to me to serve as interim pastor. After seeking God's will, I accepted the "call." In September 2009, I was installed as interim pastor and continued to serve as a humble servant to this assignment to which the Lord directed me to give leadership. Due to my declining health, I served until April 2015.

The congregation gave me a beautiful farewell banquet. We dined, worshipped God, and shared experiences with GMBC congregants, family, and friends.

In the fall of 2009, Max and I met with Reverend Ezra Bell, Jr., pastor of Fresh Start Baptist Church, and Reverend Emanuel Wasson (then pastor of Holy Trinity AME Church) to develop a community advent service. We discussed the importance of keeping Christ central for the Christmas celebration. Christ is the reason for the season. The outcome of this initial meeting was the birth of the Southern Nevada Community Advent Committee.

Southern Nevada Community Advent Pastors

Gethsemani Missionary Baptist Church Search Committee

Gethsemani's Father's Day celebration

Meeting President Obama while he was campaigning
in Las Vegas was another special moment in my life.

"For God so loved the world that He gave His only begotten Son, that whosoever believeth in Him shall not perish but have eternal life. For God did not send His Son into the world to condemn the world, but that the world through Him might be saved", John 3: 16-17.

Our journey continues on to another level. My days in ministry are filled with consulting with folks throughout the country. Max and I really enjoy the dialogue with family and friends who visit us when they are in town attending a conference, on vacation, or just stopping in Las Vegas while on their way to another destination. Sharing their ministries with us and talking about how God has used and continues to use us in their lives speaks volumes to us. Our faith in God remains strong as we continue this journey on this side of life.

Epilogue

Years have passed. Seasons have come and gone. I have more years behind me than in front of me. Then finally, the day came when I mustered enough courage to open my heart to talk about my story of survival, trust, and divine direction. As painful as it was to reopen old wounds, and dive into a lump of stuff, the idea that I will be helping somebody gave me strength. Like the lyrics from my favorite gospel song ("If I Can Help Somebody" written by Alma Irene Bazel Androzzo Thompson) goes:

If I can help somebody as I pass along,
If I can cheer somebody with a word or a song,
If I can show somebody he is travelling wrong,
Then my living shall not be in vain!

I wish I can take the credit for my well being back then and today, but the truth is every door that opened, and every decision made, was because of God. When I married my wife Maxine of 49 years, I realize now that it was the foundation God wanted me to build my life upon. Keep pace with Him.

The trolley accident was my greatest teacher. I learned that even for a three year old, life could be gone in the blink of an eye. I had two options, I could make an effort to live my life the way I had intended it to be even though I didn't have an arm, or I could allow it to bring me down. I took the spirit of courage from each of my family members and proceeded forward. I always thought I would run into the driver of that trolley but only my mom did. I wanted to tell him thank you for caring but he didn't have to feel guilt anymore because it's impossible to live in peace when you are carrying such a heavy burden. All he had to do was close his eyes and tell Jesus Christ he was sorry, ask Him to forgive him, and live under His control. My peace I give you.

For a long time, I wanted to be a singer. I was blessed with a voice and my dreams of being on a stage and having people applauding my performance was a desire of the flesh. I never thought that I would get the same response while standing in the pulpit. For 33 years, God used my voice in many ways to encourage others to never give up no matter how dim things seem. I never would have thought that being a pastor would be where I would develop my full potential. When we get into harmony with the creative power of God, there is no limitation we need to place on ourselves. He gave me clarity when I first saw St. John's Baptist Church. To most people, it looked like a gloom and doom building, but to me it was a promise of great potential.

I was blessed with intelligent parents who knew how to give advice that made you think on both sides of the issue at hand, and siblings who were just as supportive and compassionate as I was about my life's journey. But during my years as a minister, very few people had these gifts in their back pockets. I could only recall a scripture when I needed to give a solution to someone's problem, for the blueprint of life is definitely located within the pages of the Bible. More than likely it was about how

The last picture with Momma Hattie Mae. L-R: Lillian, Martha, me, and Norman. Sitting is Billy and Bob.

My siblings
in later
years:
Martha,
Norman,
Billy, and
Bob

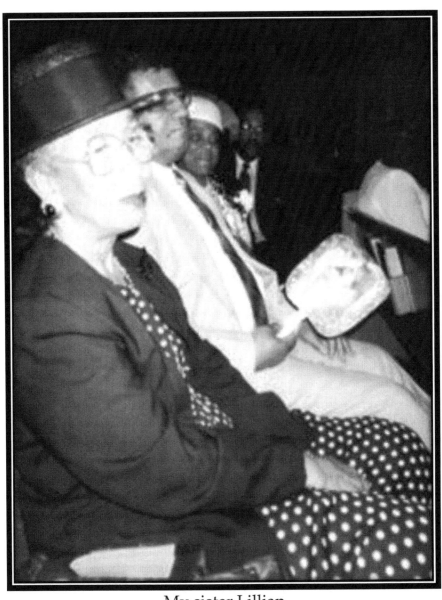

My sister Lillian

another person has done them harm. But what I do know for sure is that a person will do you more good than bad. Trust in the Lord with all thy might.

Throughout my years, and throughout my travels, no matter how strong I have been in the past, it continues to pain my heart when I think about how much I miss my mom and dad, and brothers and sisters. Recently, I lost Martha, the sister who always claimed to have been my "mom" because of our age gap. When I lost her, I lost the desire to write this book, but she was no quitter and I could hear her whisper in my ear "turn it around and finish for the sake of others who will benefit." That was enough confirmation.

Christmas
2017

I learned that a real hero is one who fights even when he is scared. I must admit, I am a little leery of what I have written and what I have forgot to write about. But I have no doubt that these moments of grandeur will do somebody's soul some good. This I promise.

Special Notes

Death
~~Life~~ Does not Hurt
Life Hurts

~~Has~~ not ~~Departed~~
Has Arrived.

Made in the USA
San Bernardino, CA
16 July 2018